CAMPING

 BOY SCOUTS OF AMERICA®

Note to the Counselor

The Camping merit badge challenges Scouts mentally and physically. Camping helps the Boy Scouts of America deliver the promise of outdoor adventure to Boy Scouts. At all times that Scouts participate in a BSA activity, they must have the proper supervision. By following the guidelines under "III. Camping" in the BSA's *Guide to Safe Scouting*, unit leaders can help ensure the well-being of Boy Scouts under their supervision. Those guidelines are discussed here briefly.

Wilderness camping. Have a plan to help minimize risks and manage a crisis should one occur. Involve Scouts and Scouters in this process so that they all know of and know how to avoid potential dangers. Camping takes proper planning, leadership, and good judgment.

Trail safety. Stay alert; take care in everything that is done on the trail, and plan activities within the group's ability and maturity level. Alert youth members to the dangers of unusual environment with proper instruction on fire safety, orienteering, and safe travel. On the trail, instruct group members to *stay together*, and avoid loose rocks and dangerous ledges, cliffs, and areas where a fall might occur. When Scouts understand the reason for rules of safety, they more willingly abide by those rules.

It is strongly recommended that at least one person in the group be currently trained in first aid through the American Red Cross or any recognized agency.

Trek Safely. Fun and safe overnight trekking activities require compliance with Trek Safely by both adult and youth leaders.

1. **Qualified supervision.** All backcountry treks must be supervised by a mature, conscientious adult at least 21 years

35866
ISBN 978-0-8395-3256-9
©2005 Boy Scouts of America
2010 Printing

BANG/Brainerd, MN
3-2010/059111

of age who understands the potential risks associated with the trek. This person knowingly accepts responsibility for the well-being and safety of the youth in his or her care.

2. **Keep fit.** Require evidence of fitness from youth and adults by having each participant fill out a current BSA Personal Health and Medical Record—Class III form. No one should participate in a trek or activity for which he or she is not physically prepared.

3. **Plan ahead.** For travel of more than 500 miles, submit the National Tour Permit Application to the local council service center at least a month before the departure date. For activities off the local council property and within 500 miles of home base, submit the Local Tour Permit Application. Units should anticipate a range of weather conditions and temperatures and develop an alternate itinerary.

4. **Gear up.** Procure topographic maps, as well as current trail maps, for the area of the trek. Take equipment and clothing that is appropriate for the weather and unit skill level, is in good condition, and is properly sized for each participant.

5. **Communicate clearly and completely.** Communication is a key to a safe outdoor adventure. Complete and share a trip plan of the trek with a contact person in the home area. At any time the itinerary changes, a leader relays the changes to the contact person, who then relays them to the Scouts' parents. The leader should carry the telephone numbers or contact information of medical and emergency services in the area of the trek. Leaders should constantly communicate with each other and the entire crew.

6. **Monitor conditions.** Leaders are responsible for making good decisions during the trek, conservatively estimating the capabilities and stamina of the group. If adverse conditions develop, the group is prepared to stop or turn back.

7. **Discipline.** Each participant knows, understands, and respects the rules and procedures for safe trekking and has been oriented in Trek Safely. Adult and youth leaders must be strict and fair, showing no favoritism.

Beware of lightning. During lightning storms, avoid the summits of mountains, crests of ridges, slopes above timberline, and large meadows. If you see a storm approaching, quickly descend to a lower elevation, away from the direction of the approaching storm. Instruct Scouts to squat down and keep their heads low. Avoid isolated trees and trees much taller than adjacent trees; and water, metal objects, and other substances that will conduct electricity over long distances.

If the threat of lightning strikes is great, group members should spread out at least 100 feet apart and squat with feet close together. Remove backpacks with either external or internal metal frames. In tents, stay away from metal poles.

Treat all drinking water. Serious illness can result from drinking or cooking with untreated water. Treat all water obtained along the trail, or carry water from home.

BSA property smart. Remember the three C's: care, courtesy, and cleanliness. Follow these guidelines:

1. In advance, obtain permission from landowners.

2. When visiting public lands, obtain a permit in advance from the land management agency.

3. Park only in designated areas.

4. If you must mark a trail, bring small signs that can be placed as the group enters and removed upon leaving.

5. Obtain permission to cross private property, and always leave gates exactly as you found them.

6. Treat the landowner's livestock and other animals with respect.

7. Keep noise to a minimum (especially at night), and follow the rules on building fires in camp.

8. Practice Leave No Trace.

9. Thank the owner as you leave, or send a thank-you note.

10. When obtaining permission to enter a property, never underestimate your departure time, and if you specify an exit time, leave at that time.

11. Do not repeatedly frequent the same sites; limit camping in the backcountry at one location to no more than three days.

12. Clean up and remove trash, and whenever possible, repair damage left by inconsiderate visitors.

Hantavirus. This deadly airborne virus is spread through contact with the urine and feces of infected rodents. Symptoms include fever, chills, muscle aches, nausea, vomiting, diarrhea, abdominal pain, and a dry, nonproductive cough. If you suspect someone has been infected, seek medical treatment immediately.

Rabies prevention. Remind Scouts to steer clear of wild animals and of domestic animals that they do not know. If someone is scratched or bitten by a potentially rabid animal, wash the wound thoroughly with soap and water. Immediately seek medical attention. Get a description of the animal, and notify local animal control officials, police, or board of health.

The guidelines mentioned here are discussed in greater detail in the *Guide to Safe Scouting,* with which all unit leaders should be familiar. Unit leaders may want to use the following BSA publications to help make campouts safer and more enjoyable.

- *Boy Scout Handbook,* 12th edition—Sections on orienteering, outdoor essentials, clothing and layering, water treatment, menus, camp cooking, and first-aid preparedness.

- *Fieldbook,* 4th edition—sections on Leadership and Trek Preparation, Leaving No Trace, Trek Adventures, and Appreciating Our Environment

- *Leave No Trace*—conservation, environmental ethics

- *Passport to High Adventure*—local council high-adventure opportunities

- *Topping Out* and *Climb On Safely*—climbing and rappelling

Requirements

1. Show that you know first aid for and how to prevent injuries or illnesses that could occur while camping, including hypothermia, frostbite, heat reactions, dehydration, altitude sickness, insect stings, tick bites, snakebite, blisters, and hyperventilation.

2. Learn the Leave No Trace principles and the Outdoor Code and explain what they mean. Write a personal and group plan for implementing these principles on your next outing.

3. Make a written plan for an overnight trek and show how to get to your camping spot using a topographical map and compass OR a topographical map and a GPS receiver. If no GPS receiver unit is available, explain how to use one to get to your camping spot.

4. Do the following:

     a. Make a duty roster showing how your patrol is organized for an actual overnight campout. List assignments for each member.

    b. Help a Scout patrol or a Webelos Scout unit in your area prepare for an actual campout, including creating the duty roster, menu planning, equipment needs, general planning, and setting up camp.

5. Do the following:

    a. Prepare a list of clothing you would need for overnight campouts in both warm and cold weather. Explain the term "layering."

    b. Discuss footwear for different kinds of weather and how the right footwear is important for protecting your feet.

c. Explain the proper care and storage of camping equipment (clothing, footwear, bedding).

d. List the outdoor essentials necessary for any campout, and explain why each item is needed.

ⓔ. Present yourself to your Scoutmaster with your pack for inspection. Be correctly clothed and equipped for an overnight campout.   AJ6

6. Do the following:

a. Describe the features of four types of tents, when and where they could be used, and how to care for tents. Working with another Scout, pitch a tent.

b. Discuss the importance of camp sanitation and tell why water treatment is essential. Then demonstrate two ways to treat water.

c. Describe the factors to be considered in deciding where to pitch your tent.

d. Tell the difference between internal- and external-frame packs. Discuss the advantages and disadvantages of each.

e. Discuss the types of sleeping bags and what kind would be suitable for different conditions. Explain the proper care of your sleeping bag and how to keep it dry. Make a comfortable ground bed.

7. Prepare for an overnight campout with your patrol by doing the following:

a. Make a checklist of personal and patrol gear that will be needed.

b. Pack your own gear and your share of the patrol equipment and food for proper carrying. Show that your pack is right for quickly getting what is needed first, and that it has been assembled properly for comfort, weight, balance, size, and neatness.

8. Do the following:

a. Explain the safety procedures for

(1) Using a propane or butane/propane stove

(2) Using a liquid fuel stove

(3) Proper storage of extra fuel

b. Discuss the advantages and disadvantages of different types of lightweight cooking stoves.

c. Prepare a camp menu. Explain how the menu would differ from a menu for a backpacking or float trip. Give recipes and make a food list for your patrol. Plan two breakfasts, three lunches, and two suppers. Discuss how to protect your food against bad weather, animals, and contamination.

d. Cook at least one breakfast, one lunch, and one dinner for your patrol from the meals you have planned for requirement 8c. At least one of those meals must be a trail meal requiring the use of a lightweight stove.

9. Show experience in camping by doing the following:

a. Camp a total of at least 20 days and 20 nights. The 20 days and 20 nights must be at a designated Scouting activity or event. Sleep each night under the sky or in a tent you have pitched. You may use a week of long-term camp toward this requirement. If the camp provides a tent that has already been pitched, you need not pitch your own tent.

ask Zack
AJ

(b) On any of these camping experiences, you must do TWO of the following, only with proper preparation and under qualified supervision.

(1) Hike up a mountain, gaining at least 1,000 vertical feet.

√(2) Backpack, snowshoe, or cross-country ski for at least 4 miles.

(3) Take a bike trip of at least 15 miles or at least four hours.

(4) Take a nonmotorized trip on the water of at least four hours or 5 miles.

√(5) Plan and carry out an overnight snow camping experience.

(6) Rappel down a rappel route of 30 feet or more.

(c.) Perform a conservation project approved by the landowner or land managing agency.

10. Discuss how the things you did to earn this badge have taught you about personal health and safety, survival, public health, conservation, and good citizenship. In your discussion, tell how Scout spirit and the Scout Oath and Law apply to camping and outdoor ethics.

Contents

Introduction

Camping! For nearly a hundred years, Scouts have been camping in open country. They have felt the sun on their backs and the wind in their faces. When storms broke overhead, they have used their skills to stay dry and warm. When a morning dawned brisk and clear, they were sure there was no better way to live.

Robert Baden-Powell knew that, as well. When he founded the Scouting movement in the early 1900s, he encouraged every Scout to learn the art of living out-of-doors. He believed a young person able to take care of himself while camping would have the confidence to meet life's other challenges, too.

Times are different now. The wonders of modern technology have shaped for us a way of life that Baden-Powell would barely recognize. But something that has not changed is the joy of going camping. Boy Scouts everywhere are still eager to head out for a night under the stars. They look forward to camping as part of longer adventures—journeys by watercraft, on foot, or saddled up to ride. When you go camping with your fellow Scouts, you have the time of your life working, playing, learning together, and enjoying one of the greatest Scouting traditions.

What Is Camping?

When the naturalist John Muir began hiking into the high
mountains of the Sierra Nevada in the 1870s, he carried little
more than bread or crackers, some grain meal, and a bit of
sugar and tea. He had several cans he could use as pots. At
night he rolled up in a couple of blankets and built a fire to
keep warm. With his light load, Muir ranged far and wide
among the rugged California peaks.

Today, members of a Scout troop in a small Midwestern
town hike through farm fields and along dusty roads to a patch
of woods where they settle in for the night. Scouts from a com-
munity in the mountains climb a steep trail to an alpine lake,
their backpacks filled with just the right gear for a wilderness
trek. A Scout patrol makes itself comfortable for an exciting
week of long-term camping at a favorite council camp. On foot,
in canoes, rafts, and sailboats, or with strings of pack animals,
expeditions of older Scouts set off on challenging itineraries at
BSA high-adventure bases across the country. And every four or
five years, Boy Scouts by the thousands gather for the national
Scout jamboree. They pitch their tents in circles or rows, cook
their own meals, and spend their days building friendships and
sampling a wide range of Scouting skills and events.

John Muir *was* camping. So are all of these Scouts.
Camping is such a wide-open activity that it has room for
everyone, from 10 backpackers moving lightly through a
wilderness area to 10,000 Scouts pitching their tents in
campsites reachable by a road.

Scouts setting off on camping trips share an eagerness
to live simply and well, and to put the values of Scouting
in motion by doing all they can to protect the
environment they are privileged to enjoy.

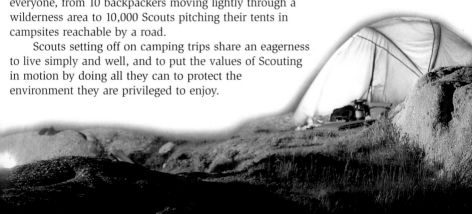

Preparation

Of all that you can take with you on a camping trip, the most important thing is knowledge. Plan ahead and you can be fairly sure that you will have everything you need—both in your pack and in your head—to make a camping trip a success. Start by thinking about how you will manage risk.

Risk Management

Risk management is so much a part of camping that we often don't notice we are doing it. When we fill bottles with water from streams and lakes, we deal with the potential risk of parasites by treating the water with a filter, boiling it, or using chemical treatment. When we share the backcountry with bears, we protect them and ourselves by hanging our food out of their reach, eliminating odors from our sleeping areas, and keeping campsites spotless. When foul weather blows in, routes become uncomfortably exposed, streams swell, or snow loads make avalanches a possibility, we make decisions that keep risks at acceptable levels.

Perhaps the greatest risk to be managed in the backcountry is also one of its real attractions—the simple matter of distance. The farther you travel from clinics, physicians, and rescue squads, the more you must rely upon yourself and your companions to maintain your safety. Of course, the best response to risk is to avoid it. That requires good planning, leadership, and an awareness of your surroundings so that you can make wise decisions every step of the way.

The more responsibility every Scout takes for personal health and safety, the more each of you can contribute to a successful camping trip. You also will be in a stronger position to provide assistance if an emergency does arise. Here are some ways you can increase your role in risk management:

- Stay in good physical shape so you are ready for the demands of camping.
- Know where you are going and what to expect.
- Adjust clothing layers to match changing conditions.
- Drink plenty of water.
- Protect yourself from exposure to the sun, to biting insects, and to poisonous plants.
- Take care of your gear.

Lastly, let others know when you are having difficulties or are aware of a concern that might affect you or the group. Stopping for a few moments to deal with a hot spot on a heel can help avoid bringing the group to a long halt later in the day when blisters break out. Speaking up about changes you notice in the weather or asking questions you have about whether a campsite is appropriate can help everyone make the best decisions.

First-Aid Preparedness

Managing risk includes being prepared to handle emergencies that might occur. Camping can take you far from urban areas where emergency medical care is close by. In the field, your group might need to care for an injured or ill person for a few hours or even a day or more until help arrives. That requires thinking about first aid in different ways than you would when you are in a city.

Completing the first-aid requirements for the Tenderfoot, Second Class, and First Class Scout ranks can help you prepare to deal with illnesses and injuries that could arise while you are camping. So can earning the First Aid merit badge. The current editions of the *Boy Scout Handbook* and *Fieldbook* include descriptions of the symptoms and treatment of hypothermia, heatstroke, heat exhaustion, frostbite, dehydration, sunburn, insect stings, tick bites, snakebite, and blisters. In addition, familiarize yourself with the symptoms, prevention, and treatment of altitude sickness, hyperventilation, asthma, and food allergies.

Altitude Sickness

Camping may take you to high places where altitude sickness (also known as AMS, or acute mountain sickness) can be a concern. Fortunately, altitude sickness is seldom a problem for people at elevations of less than 8,000 feet above sea level.

Going to a place that is higher than you are accustomed may leave you short of breath because the atmosphere around you becomes thinner and contains less oxygen. Within a few days your body will acclimate to higher altitudes by producing extra red blood cells to carry more oxygen to your tissues and organs, and you should feel fine.

Taking steps to help prevent altitude sickness is far better than suffering from it during a camping trip. The following suggestions can make your alpine adventures more comfortable and more fun, too.

- Drink plenty of fluids. As a rule, take in enough water so that your urine remains clear rather than dark yellow.

- Give your body time to acclimate gradually as you go higher. Spend a few days at 5,000 to 7,000 feet and then a few more at 8,000 to 10,000 feet.

- "Climb high, sleep low." Use this mountaineer's trick for acclimating by hiking upward during the day and then descending to a lower camp for a good night's rest.

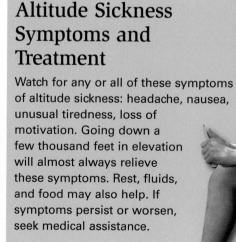

Altitude Sickness Symptoms and Treatment

Watch for any or all of these symptoms of altitude sickness: headache, nausea, unusual tiredness, loss of motivation. Going down a few thousand feet in elevation will almost always relieve these symptoms. Rest, fluids, and food may also help. If symptoms persist or worsen, seek medical assistance.

Hypothermia

The symptoms of altitude sickness also can be warning signs of hypothermia. Begin treatment for hypothermia by making sure that the person is warm, is wearing dry clothing, is sheltered from the wind and chilly or wet weather, and has had enough to eat and drink. If the person does not rapidly improve and the elevation is above 8,000 feet, treat for altitude sickness as well.

Hyperventilation

Stress and anxiety about outdoor adventures can sometimes cause a person to suffer from hyperventilation—quick, shallow breathing that can upset the balance of oxygen and carbon dioxide in the body. Someone experiencing hyperventilation can become light-headed, faint, and sometimes feel tingling or numbness in the fingers and toes.

Treating Hyperventilation. The symptoms of hyperventilation usually will go away if the person relaxes and slows his breathing. Removing the causes of his anxiety is important, too, either by moving to a different location or by talking through the situation. Extensive or repeated episodes of hyperventilation might be signs of other medical concerns and should be checked out by a physician.

Managing Asthma and Allergic Reactions

Asthma and allergies are seldom barriers for Scouts to participate fully in troop campouts. For example, if a Scout is severely allergic to peanuts, his troop can operate as a peanut-free zone during meetings and camping trips. That will create a safe environment for everyone and will show the values of Scouting in action by making opportunities for adventures available to everyone.

Scouts who have asthma or allergies to certain foods, bee stings, or other agents must let group leaders know ahead of time the exact nature of their situation and how they should be treated for an asthma attack or an allergic reaction. They also should consult with their physicians to prepare themselves for outdoor activities with strategies and treatment kits, and should share that information with their group leaders.

Leave No Trace and the Outdoor Code

From the Appalachians to the Cascades, and from the Gulf Coast to the Great Lakes, America is blessed with magnificent open country. As a camper, you will have many chances to enjoy America's expanses, but with that privilege comes a great responsibility to cause no harm to the environment.

The BSA has adopted the principles of Leave No Trace to help Scouts enjoy their experience to the fullest, but in ways that protect the areas where they travel. The rewards of leaving no trace are well worth learning new skills. The future of unspoiled territory—and the continuing opportunity to visit it depends in large part on how responsibly Scouts today conduct themselves.

In order to write a personal and group plan for implementing these principles on a camping trip, become familiar with the seven principles of Leave No Trace.

The Principles of Leave No Trace

1. Plan ahead and prepare.

   - In advance, obtain information concerning geography and weather, and plan accordingly.

   - Know the regulations and special concerns of the area you'll visit, and keep your group's size within allowed limits.

   - Allow enough time to reach your destination.

   - Go to areas appropriate for your activities and skill level.

2. Travel and camp on durable surfaces.

   - Durable surfaces include established trails and campsites, rock, gravel, dry grasses, and snow.

   - Protect areas near water by camping at least 200 feet from lakes and streams.

   - Good campsites are found, not made. Altering a site is not necessary.

   - In popular areas, use existing trails and campsites. Walk single file in the middle of the trail, even when it is wet or muddy. Keep campsites small. Focus activity in areas where vegetation is absent. In pristine areas, spread out to prevent the creation of campsites and trails. Avoid places where impacts are just beginning.

3. Dispose of waste properly (pack it in, pack it out).

- Pack it in, pack it out. Inspect your campsite and rest areas for trash or spilled foods. Pack out all trash, leftover food, and litter.

- Deposit solid human waste in catholes dug 6 to 8 inches deep at least 200 feet from water, camp, and trails. Cover and disguise the cathole when finished.

- Where necessary, pack out toilet paper and hygiene products.

- To wash yourself or your dishes, carry water 200 feet away from streams or lakes and use small amounts of biodegradable soap. Scatter strained dishwater.

4. Leave what you find.

- Preserve the past; examine, but do not touch, cultural or historic structures and artifacts.

- Do not pick plants or disturb natural settings, animals, and archaeological artifacts. Enjoy them where they are. (It may be illegal to remove or disturb wildlife and artifacts.)

- Leave rocks, plants, and other natural objects as you find them.

- Do not dig trenches or build lean-tos, tables, or chairs.

5. Minimize campfire impacts.

- Campfires can cause lasting impacts to the backcountry. Use a lightweight stove for cooking and enjoy a candle lantern for light.

- Where fires are permitted, use established fire rings.

- Keep fires small. Only use sticks from the ground that can be broken by hand.

- Burn all wood and coals to ash, put out campfires completely, then scatter cool ashes.

6. Respect wildlife.

- Observe wildlife from a distance. Do not approach them.

- Never feed animals. Feeding them damages their health, alters natural behaviors, and exposes them to predators and other dangers.

• Protect wildlife and your food by storing rations and trash securely.

• Avoid wildlife during sensitive times: mating, nesting, raising young, and enduring winter.

7. Be considerate of other visitors.

• Respect other visitors' privacy and property.

• Be courteous. Yield to other users on the trail.

• Camp away from trails and other visitors.

• Let nature's sounds prevail. Keep the noise down.

The Outdoor Code

The Outdoor Code of the Boy Scouts of America reminds Scouts of the importance of caring for the environment. The code's ideals have special meaning whenever you are camping, hiking, or taking part in other outdoor events.

Outdoor Code
As an American, I will do my best to—
Be clean in my outdoor manners,
Be careful with fire,
Be considerate in the outdoors, and
Be conservation-minded.

Where to Camp

With Leave No Trace principles and the Outdoor Code in mind, consider where you want to camp. Your choice of a campsite depends upon what you want to do and see, how much time you have, and the kind of camping that appeals to you.

Frontcountry Camping

Frontcountry sites are those that can easily be reached by automobile, public transit, or bicycle. Frontcountry camping locations include campgrounds in national, state, and local parks and forests; property owned by the BSA; and, with permission, many private lands. Developed campgrounds may have designated tent sites and fireplaces, public rest rooms, and sources of clean drinking water.

Because these sites are usually near roads, Scouts taking part in frontcountry camping often can carry more gear and provisions than they might on trips that require backpacking. Meals can include fresh ingredients and involve more elaborate preparation, such as baking in Dutch ovens.

Frontcountry camping is ideal for Scouts learning the basics of living out-of-doors. With several frontcountry campouts under their belts, they will have a much better idea of what to carry when they travel farther from the road, and how to manage camps at more remote destinations.

Concentrate camp activity in high-use areas such as this frontcountry campsite.

BSA Summer Camp

A highlight of the year for many Scout troops is a week at a BSA summer camp. It is rare for a Scout to come home without having gained more knowledge about living in the out-of-doors and great enthusiasm for doing more of it as soon as possible.

Backcountry Camping

The nature of a camping trip changes dramatically when you leave the road behind and venture into the backcountry. Everything you need for a night or more must be carried in a pack on your back, stowed in duffels tied into a canoe, or loaded onto a horse, burro, or mule. As you leave civilization behind, a great world of possibilities and responsibilities opens before you.

Backcountry camping can take you to places that few people ever reach. You can spend time near remote lakes, in deep forests, and in desert terrain. Best of all, you can rely on your own skill and determination to make the most of living for a while beyond the usual bounds of civilization.

BSA High-Adventure Bases

BSA high-adventure bases feature backcountry camping adventures. Designed for older Boy Scouts, Varsity Scouts, and Venturers, each high-adventure base of the BSA's National Council offers the training, equipment, and support you need to set out on wilderness treks that will challenge your skills, strength, and willpower.

Scouts at Philmont Scout Ranch can embark on backpacking treks into the high country of northern New Mexico. Expeditions from the bases of the Northern Tier National High Adventure Program paddle canoes along the lakes and rivers of the Boundary Waters of northern Minnesota and southern Ontario and Manitoba in Canada. Headquartered in the Florida Keys, the Florida National High Adventure Sea Base is the starting point for oceangoing expeditions that include camping on the islands and distant coastlines of the Keys and the Bahamas.

Many BSA local councils have their own high-adventure bases. Among the activities they may offer older Scouts are backpacking, camping, rock climbing, canoeing, and river rafting.

Visit a directory of the high-adventure bases located across the nation at *http://www. scouting.org/ scoutsource/ Applications/ highadventure search.aspx*

Trip Plan

Trip plan of _____

Where
Destination _____
Route going _____

Route returning _____

When
Date and time of departure _____
Date and time of return _____

Who
Names of participants _____

Why
Purpose of the trip _____

What
- ☑ Gear and other items to be taken:
- ☐ Outdoor Essentials
- ☐ Other clothing and gear _____

Permits required _____
Special equipment needs _____
Special clothing needs _____

How
List the principles of Leave No Trace that relate to your trip. For each one, write a sentence explaining what the patrol will do to follow that principle. _____

Trip Plan

Wherever you decide to camp, you will need to prepare a written trip plan. Well before your departure, share the plan with your Scout leaders and parents or guardian. They may have suggestions that will make your time in the outdoors even better. A trip plan also will let the leaders know where you will be and will enable them to provide support if it is needed.

Include the following information in your trip plan:

- Where you are going
- From where and when you will depart
- How you will reach the camp
- What you will be doing
- Who is going along
- When you will return
- When and how you will obtain permits or permission required by land management agencies or landowners of the places you wish to travel and camp
- A brief emergency response plan that includes the location and telephone number of the clinic or hospital closest to your camp and route of travel, the phone number of the local emergency response authority (in most areas, 911), and the name of the person in your group who will take charge in an emergency.

Scout troops and patrols sometimes attach gear lists, menus, and duty rosters to their trip plans. With all the paperwork together, patrol leaders can more easily assign to various Scouts the tasks of gathering equipment, shopping for food, and taking care of the other details of preparing for a camping trip.

Menus

Camping builds big appetites. With planning and practice, you can match that hunger with mouth-watering meals sure to keep you and your crew going strong all day.

When the key activities of an adventure take place away from your campsite—rappelling, for example, or conservation projects, float trips, canoeing, or wildlife photography—make meal preparation quick and easy so that you can get back to the action as soon as possible. On more leisurely campouts, cooking can take center stage. In stormy weather, there is no better way to pass the time than firing up the camp stove and fixing something good to eat.

Dried/Dehydrated Foods

Much of the weight of many foods is water. Remove it, and the result is a selection of lightweight ingredients just right for campers. Most grocery stores carry pow-dered milk, instant cocoa, dehydrated potatoes and other vegetables, soup mixes, and many other dried foods. Some camping stores sell entire camp meals that require only the addition of boiling water.

Keep these suggestions in mind as you plan meals for a camping trip:

- Select foods that will not spoil. In the frontcountry, you may be able to bring fresh fruits and vegetables, and keep meat and dairy products safe in a cooler with ice. For backcountry treks, depend more upon grains, pastas, and dehydrated or dried ingredients.

- When you camp in the frontcountry or travel by watercraft or with pack animals, the weight of your food may not be a critical factor. Besides taking items that are fresh or canned, you might be able to include additional cooking gear, too— a Dutch oven for stews and baking desserts, for example, or a griddle for a big breakfast of flapjacks, bacon, and eggs.

- Trim the weight of your backpack by eliminating water from your provisions. Grains, pastas, cereals, and dried or dehydrated fruits, vegetables, soup mixes, and sauces provide plenty of punch per pound.

- Repackage food in resealable plastic bags to reduce clutter and weight. On a piece of tape attached to each bag, write the contents of the bag and the meal for which it will be used.

Cook Safely!

The first item involved in safe cooking is, of course, the food. Meats and dairy foods must be kept cold during storage, and once meat is removed from its protective wrapper, the cook must take care to keep it separate from other food items. Because bacteria can grow in meat, the meat must be cooked thoroughly as soon as it is no longer kept cold. Likewise, any uneaten, cooked meat must be properly stored and kept cold to eliminate the risk of growing bacteria. (For more information on protecting food from contamination, see the *Cooking* merit badge pamphlet.)

Menu and Recipe Ideas

Once you know how many meals you need, write down what you want to prepare and eat for each of those meals. The menus and recipes here will give you some ideas. Other ideas might come from your parents, other Scouts in your patrol, the *Boy Scout Handbook, Fieldbook,* or the *Cooking* merit badge pamphlet.

SAMPLE MENUS

Trail breakfast: instant hot cereal, mixed dried fruits, cocoa

Camp breakfast: pancakes, apple, milk or orange juice

RECIPE FOR INSTANT PANCAKES

- Pancake mix ("complete" variety that needs only water)
- Large resealable bag

Before leaving for camp, measure the necessary amount of pancake mix in a plastic bag. On the bag, write how much water to add. At camp, add water, seal the bag, knead to mix, and pour in small dollops from the bag onto the hot griddle. Watch the pancakes closely. When the small bubbles at the edges of the pancake begin to burst, turn the pancakes. Continue until you have as many pancakes as needed. Save leftover pancake batter by carefully resealing the bag for later use (and placing it in a cooler).

Trail lunch: peanut butter and jelly sandwich, carrot sticks, chocolate pudding, juice (canned or boxed)

Camp lunch: hot dogs with condiments (pickle, relish, mustard, ketchup) pork 'n' beans, sliced pears, chocolate milk

Camp lunch: tomato soup, grilled ham and cheese sandwich with pickles on the side, corn chips, apple juice

Trail dinner: instant chicken and rice soup, heated sliced beef on wheat rolls, carrot sticks, milk

Camp dinner: black bean soup, Texas hash, lettuce and tomato salad, fried bananas, milk

RECIPE FOR TEXAS HASH

1 tablespoon cooking oil

1 pound ground meat

1 large onion, chopped

1 medium bell pepper, chopped

Garlic powder, to taste

1 8-ounce can stewed tomatoes

1 teaspoon chili powder

1 cup cooked rice

Salt, pepper to taste

Grated Monterey Jack or cheddar cheese, optional

In a Dutch oven, heat oil over the campfire or stove and brown the meat, stirring to break up chunks. Set meat aside on a plate. Add onion, bell pepper, and garlic powder to pan. Cook just until tender. Add tomatoes, tomato sauce, meat, and chili powder; mix well. Add rice, season to taste. Bake until hot, 20 to 25 minutes. Sprinkle grated cheese on top during the last five minutes of baking.

Duty Roster

Cooperation keeps a camp running smoothly. So does having one or two people in charge of each essential activity. A duty roster lists the work that needs to be done and assigns tasks to each member of a group. During long-term camping, Scouts can switch chores each day after lunch. On overnight outings, each Scout can perform one duty, then take on a different responsibility for the next campout.

A typical duty roster might break camp tasks into these tasks:

• **Water and stoves.** Maintain the water supply for cooking and cleanup. Establish a safe place for stoves to be fueled and used, and have them ready to light before the cooks need them.

• **Cooking.** Assemble ingredients and follow recipes to prepare and serve meals. Have wash water heating on the stove before serving meals.

• **Cleanup.** Set out wash and rinse water, oversee the washing of group cooking gear, stow pots and utensils, and dispose of garbage. (For more on washing dishes in camp, see the *Boy Scout Handbook* and *Fieldbook.*)

• **Food storage.** Maintain a bear line or other food storage system to protect provisions from animals and weather. Secure all food items at night and whenever camp will be left unattended.

Many groups also develop a list of assignments to be completed before a camping trip begins. Duties may include:

• Assembling crew equipment

• Developing menus, shopping for food, and repackaging provisions

• Getting maps and planning routes

• Securing permits or other forms of permission

Gearing Up

Each outdoor adventure is different, and the equipment you take may change from one camping trip to the next. For times when you want to travel light and move quickly through the backcountry, pack exactly what is required for safety and comfort, but not an ounce more. On other campouts, especially those requiring little or no foot travel to reach the site, you may want to add extras to enhance the pleasure of your time in the out-of-doors.

Personal Gear

Use the following checklists as reminders of the gear and clothing you and your group may want to pack for a camping trip. Beyond the outdoor essentials, you might not need every item every time. By considering everything on each list, though, you can decide whether something will be useful, and you will be less likely to forget what could turn out to be an important piece of clothing or equipment for the trip you are about to begin.

Outdoor Essentials

Pocketknife. Cut a cord, trim a bandage, slice some cheese, tighten a screw on a camp stove—a pocketknife is the all-purpose tool for the out-of-doors.

First-aid kit. Carrying a few first-aid items in a self-sealing plastic bag will allow you to treat scratches, blisters, and other minor injuries, and to provide initial care if more serious emergencies arise.

Extra clothing and rain gear. Weather conditions in the outdoors can change quickly. Have the clothing you need to deal with extremes of weather—heat, cold, and storm.

Water bottle. The amount of water you need to carry depends on the activities of the day and the sources of water you will encounter. While heat and humidity can make you more thirsty, it is very important to drink plenty of fluids in cold weather, too.

Flashlight. A flashlight will help you set up camp in the dark or find your way home after the sun has gone down. Carry spare batteries and an extra bulb.

Trail food. You'll burn a lot of energy in the outdoors. A stash of nuts, raisins, and dried fruits will help keep you going, especially if a trip lasts longer than expected.

Matches and fire starters. Camp without relying on an open fire, but be prepared to build one in an emergency by carrying several fire starters that are reliable, durable, and protected from the elements.

Sun protection. Sunburn is a common injury in the outdoors. Repeated burns can cause long-term damage and skin cancer. Wear sunscreen with an SPF of at least 15.

Map and compass. Use them to find your way through unfamiliar terrain, when visibility is poor, and where expected trail signs are missing.

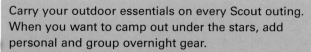

Carry your outdoor essentials on every Scout outing. When you want to camp out under the stars, add personal and group overnight gear.

Personal Overnight Camping Gear

☐ Clothing for the season (see box for warm- and cold-weather camping)

☐ Backpack

☐ Rain cover for backpack

☐ Sleeping bag, or two or three blankets

☐ Ground cloth and pad

☐ Eating kit: spoon, plate, bowl, cup

☐ Cleanup kit: soap, toothbrush, toothpaste, dental floss, comb, washcloth, towel

☐ Personal extras (optional): watch, camera and film, notebook, pencil or pen, sunglasses, small musical instrument, swimsuit, gloves

Group Overnight Camping Gear

☐ Tents with poles, stakes, ground cloths, and lines

☐ Dining fly

☐ Nylon cord, 50 feet

☐ Backpacking stoves and fuel

☐ Cook kit: pots and pans, spatula, large spoon and/or ladle, plastic sheets (two 4-by-4-foot), matches and/or butane lighters in waterproof containers

☐ Cleanup kit: sponge or dishcloth, biodegradable soap, sanitizing rinse agent (bleach), scouring pads (no-soap type), plastic trash bags, toilet paper in plastic bag

☐ Repair kit: thread, needles, safety pins

☐ Group extras (optional): hot-pot tongs, camp shovel, plastic water container, washbasin, grill, pot rods, patrol flag, small U.S. flag, ax, camp saw

Clothing Checklist

For Warm-Weather Camping:

- T-shirt or short-sleeved shirt (lightweight)
- Hiking shorts
- Underwear
- Socks
- Long-sleeved shirt (lightweight)
- Long pants (lightweight)
- Sweater or warm jacket
- Brimmed hat
- Bandannas
- Rain gear

For Cold-Weather Camping:

- Long-sleeved shirt
- Long pants (fleece or wool)
- Sweater (fleece or wool)
- Long underwear (polypropylene)
- Socks (wool or synthetic blend)
- Warm hooded parka or jacket
- Stocking hat (fleece or wool)
- Mittens or gloves (fleece or wool) with water-resistant shells
- Wool scarf
- Rain gear

Layering

For the most comfort in the outdoors with the least weight in your pack, use the layering system. Choose layers of clothing that, when combined, will meet the most extreme weather you expect to encounter. On a chilly autumn day, for example, you might set out from the trailhead wearing long pants, a wool shirt, a fleece sweater, mittens, and a stocking hat. As you hike, the effort will cause your body to generate heat. Peel off the sweater and stuff it in your pack. Still too warm? Loosen a few buttons on your shirt or slip off your mittens and hat.

You also can use layering to keep cool in hot climates by stripping down to hiking shorts, a T-shirt, and a brimmed hat. Lightweight long pants and a long-sleeved shirt will shield you from insects, brush, and the sun.

Footwear for Camping

Almost any durable shoes will do for a frontcountry camping trip. When your plans include walking to a backcountry campsite with all your food and gear in your pack, hiking boots can give your feet and ankles protection and support.

In addition to boots for hiking, you might want to carry a pair of running shoes or other comfortable, lightweight shoes to wear around camp. Any shoes or boots you use for camping must fit well. Your heels should not slip much when you walk, and your toes should have a little wiggle room.

Clean your boots or shoes after every outing. Use a stiff brush to remove mud, or wash them off with water and mild soap, then allow footwear to dry at room temperature. (Placing shoes too close to a campfire can dry out leather and damage nylon.) The manufacturers of leather boots might recommend treatment with a boot dressing or waterproofing agent; follow their instructions.

> Be sure to break in new boots before using them in the field. Wear them several times, gradually extending the length of time you wear them, until they feel like a natural part of your feet.

Sleeping Bag

On clear summer nights, a ground bed made up with a blanket or two may provide all the warmth you need. For most camping, though, a sleeping bag is the way to go. The outer fabric of a sleeping bag is called the shell. Usually made of nylon, it can shield you from gusts of wind and may be treated by the manufacturer to repel dew and light mist.

Contained within the shell is an insulating fill material that traps your body warmth and holds it close to you. Thin fabric walls called baffles are sewn into the shell to keep the fill material spaced evenly throughout the bag.

The warmest fill material per ounce is goose down—the fluffy underfeathers of waterfowl. Explorers, mountaineers, and campers through the decades have relied on down when they expected to sleep out in the cold. Down bags are expensive, cannot keep you warm when they are wet, and are difficult to dry in camp unless the sun comes out. With all of that in mind, it's still a fact that down bags are good when campers want to travel as lightly as possible and have the experience to keep their bags dry.

Synthetic fill can be almost as light as goose down, but it seldom is as costly. Its greatest advantage is that it can keep you warm even when your sleeping bag gets wet. You will, of course, be much more comfortable in a dry synthetic-fill bag than in a wet one, so don't be careless with it in stormy weather.

The useful life of any sleeping bag can be extended if you remove it from its stuff sack between trips. Store it by hanging it in a closet or by placing it loosely in a large cotton laundry bag. That will prevent the fill material from being overly compressed, and circulating air will help keep the bag fresh.

Sleeping Pad. Increase your comfort at night with a sleeping pad. Made of foam, a pad will give you a soft surface on which to lie and will prevent the cold earth beneath you from drawing away your body heat. Foam pads are often lighter and more durable than air mattresses, and they insulate better.

Ground Cloth. Keep moisture away from your bedding with a ground cloth—a plastic sheet cut to the size of your sleeping bag or tent floor. Tuck the edges of the ground cloth beneath the floor of your tent so that rainwater will not collect on the cloth and run under the tent.

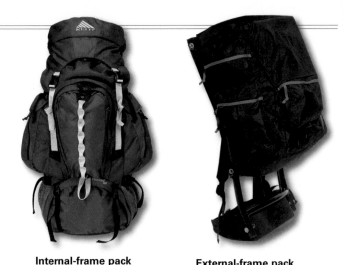

Internal-frame pack   **External-frame pack**

When shopping for a new backpack, ask the store clerk to load it with 20 to 30 pounds of weight. Swing it onto your shoulders, adjust it for a comfortable fit, then carry it around the store for a while to get a feel for it. That will help you know when you have found the right pack for you.

Pack

Packs can be either external or internal framed. Many people feel that packs with internal frames fit better. Streamlined, compact shapes make these packs good for use while skiing, climbing, and traveling cross-country. They fit more easily into canoes than do packs with external frames. External-frame packs are popular among Scouts who prefer them for backpacking along open trails or for carrying heavy loads.

ADJUSTABLE STRAP

PAD EXTENDS JUST BELOW CHEST

LOW PRESSURE ON SHOULDER

BELT ON HIP REST

No Fires in Tents

Keep all flames away from tents. Never use candles, matches, stoves, heaters, or lanterns in or near tents. No tent is fireproof. All of them can burn or melt when exposed to heat. Use flashlights only!

Tents

The development of synthetic fabrics has opened a new era of possibilities for tent designers. Nylon and breathable fabrics lend themselves to roomy shelters that pack small and weigh little. Flexible poles made of aluminum or fiberglass make possible geometric tent shapes that stand up to tremendous amounts of wind, rain, and snow. A ground cloth underneath the tent floor protects it from abrasion and provides an added barrier to moisture.

Most tents used by Scouts today have a tent body made of breathable nylon. The tent body is shielded from rain, snow, and wind by a waterproof rain fly. Moisture created by people breathing inside the tent passes through the tent body, keeping the interior dry and comfortable.

Because of the great variety of tents on the market today, be sure you follow the manufacturer's instructions on how to pitch your tent. Practice pitching your tent before you go camping. Here are a few tips for pitching a tent:

- At the campsite, choose a level site that drains well.

- Remove stones and large sticks, but try not to disturb the natural ground cover.

- Spread out a ground cloth to protect the tent floor from dirt, sharp objects, and moisture.

- Unfold the tent on top of the ground cloth. Pull out the corners of the floor and stake them to the ground, then assemble the poles and put them in place.

- Use taut-line hitches to tie the free ends of guylines around stakes you have pushed into the ground, and pull the lines tight.

- Put a rain fly over the tent and stake it down.

Modern tents are often rated as three-season (good for spring, summer, and autumn use) or four-season (reliable in any conditions, including winter camping). Four-season tents may have additional poles and more durable fabric, thus making them sturdier but heavier.

Common Tent Shapes

Tarps. The simplest of all tents, a tarp can be pitched in many ways—as a lean-to, for instance, or a pyramid, or a pup tent. The advantages of a tarp are its light weight and versatility. However, it has no floor, offers little protection against insects, and must be pitched well in order to protect campers from rain. Tarps often are used as dining flies to shelter group cook sites.

A-Frames. Seen from the front, this tent is shaped like the letter A, thus its name. Most A-frame tents are equipped with mosquito netting, a rain fly, and a waterproof floor.

Tarp

A-frame tent

Hybrid tent

Dome tent

Domes. Tents with a dome shape can be spacious with lots of headroom. The arrangement of poles bending over the tent body gives a dome plenty of stability, even in strong winds. Domes are often freestanding—requiring no tent stakes. Since dome tents are usually larger than A-frames, they also can weigh more.

Hybrids. Mix geometry, modern materials, and the imagina-
tions of tent makers, and you get an astounding variety of
shapes. Among the most interesting are hybrid tents that
combine features of A-frames and domes. Some look like
rounded A-frames, tunnels, or domes cut in half. Doors may
be at the ends, or sewn into one or both sides. Many include
a vestibule—a porchlike extension of the rain fly that provides
shelter outside the tent body for storing packs, crew gear, and
muddy boots.

Breathable Tents

Lots of rain gear today is made of fabric that protects you from
precipitation and, at the same time, allows moisture given off
by your body to escape. The same material is sometimes used
to make tents. Because they do not need a rain fly, these single-
wall breathable tents are lightweight yet strong enough to stand
harsh conditions. On the other hand, they are usually small,
can be clammy in warm weather, and may be very expensive.

Never dig ditches around your tent; they leave scars on the ground that can take a long time to heal.

Wall tent

Wall Tents

For long-term, frontcountry outings such as a week at a BSA
council camp, your group may use wall tents. Large enough
for several Scouts to unroll their sleeping bags on the floor or
on cots, modern wall tents are constructed of canvas, a polyes-
ter-cotton blend, or nylon. A ridgepole running between two
upright poles holds the tent erect. Windows or the side walls of
many large tents can be opened in hot weather to allow interior
ventilation. Most wall tents are too heavy and cumbersome for
use on backcountry campouts.

Tent Care

- Take off your boots before crawling into a tent. Stocking feet are kinder to tent floors, and you won't track in mud. Store your boots by the tent door, under the shelter of the rain fly.

- The stitched seams in the rain flies of new tents may need to be sealed to prevent moisture from leaking through. New tents usually include seam sealer and the manufacturer's instructions for applying it.

- Tent fabric can be harmed by too much exposure to sunlight. Of course, your tent may be set up in a sunny place for a day or two during a campout, but try to avoid leaving it pitched in the open when it is not in use or when you can put it in a shaded campsite instead.

- Clean out your tent by sweeping it or, if it is small, by tipping it up and shaking out litter and debris.

- To stow a tent in a storage sack, first place the bundle of collapsed poles in the tent's stuff sack. Next, push a corner of the tent all the way to the bottom of the sack. Continue stuffing the fabric alongside the poles.

- A tent that seems dry in camp may have absorbed dew or ground moisture. For that reason, it is important that you always unpack your tent when you get home and set it up, hang it over a clothesline, or suspend it from nails in the rafters of a shed or basement. Allow it to dry completely before storing it.

Stoves

For much of Scouting's history, no campout was complete without a wood fire. Scouts prided themselves on their ability to kindle a blaze in any conditions, even in a rainstorm. They used fires to cook their meals and, in the evenings, as the center of a camp's activities.

There are times when a campfire is still appropriate, and there are campsites where open fires will do little or no harm. However, Scouts today are wiser in knowing when not to build a fire. Through Leave No Trace, they understand that fires can leave scars on the land, blackening stones and sterilizing soil. Lighting campfires in heavily used campsites can mar surrounding forests as people gather up every stick of dead wood and break off tree branches for fuel.

Instead, most Scout campers now use stoves for cooking, and that means they can prepare meals where there is little firewood or none at all. With camp stoves, they can make themselves comfortable in nearly every sort of weather and on almost any terrain.

Selecting a Stove

The stove you choose depends upon the kind of cooking you will do, the type of fuel you wish to use, and the amount of weight you are willing to carry. Of the many stoves on the market, those burning the following fuels are most useful in camp. Always read and follow the manufacturer's instructions for carrying, fueling, using, and storing camp stoves.

Carefully follow stove manufacturers' instructions when selecting fuel. Some stoves operate only with white gas, while others also burn unleaded gasoline, kerosene, or even jet fuel.

White Gas. White gas is a highly distilled fuel used in many North American backpacking stoves. Some white gas stoves must be preheated, often by squeezing a dab of flammable paste into a depression at the base of the burner stem. Preheating increases the pressure inside the fuel tank, forcing vaporized fuel up a stem and into a burner where it can be ignited with a match. Once the burner is roaring, it will keep the fuel tank hot enough to maintain a steady supply of vaporized fuel.

More advanced white gas stoves are equipped with pumps to pressurize their fuel tanks. That can be a real advantage in cold weather.

Cartridge Stoves. Simplicity, safety, and convenience are features of butane and propane cartridge stoves. Cartridge stoves need no pumping or preheating; simply attach a fuel canister, turn the control knob, and light the burner. Cartridge stoves work well in warm weather and at high altitudes, but they lose efficiency as the temperature drops.

Cartridge stove

Propane Tank Stoves. Two-burner propane stoves are too heavy for backpacking but can be just right for larger groups on river rafting expeditions and for Scout groups camping close to a road.

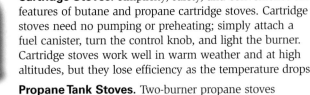

Propane tank stove

Kerosene. Kerosene is a hot-burning, nonexplosive fuel available almost anywhere in the world. While kerosene camping stoves are unusual in North America, they are a familiar sight on international expeditions. A kerosene stove must be preheated before it can be lit.

Using Stoves Safely

Stoves of different designs operate in different ways. Before lighting any stove, read and understand the manufacturer's instructions. Then follow the instructions exactly. In addition, *always* heed these stove safety rules:

1. Never use a stove inside or near a tent.

2. Don't overload a stove with a heavy pot. Instead, set up a grill over the stove to bear the weight of the pot.

3. Never leave a burning stove unattended.

4. Let a stove cool completely before you put it away. (In preparation for long-term storage—a month or more—empty the fuel tank.)

5. Do not open the fuel cap of a hot stove or attempt to refuel a hot stove.

6. Store liquid fuel only in well-marked metal fuel bottles designed specifically for that use.

7. Even if they are empty, keep fuel bottles and canisters away from sources of heat.

8. Reduce fire danger at home by storing all fuel containers in a shed, garage, or other uninhabited structure, not inside your house.

Cook Kits and Utensils

As you plan meals for a campout, list the pots and pans you will need for preparing each dish. Your list might include a frying pan and pots of various sizes, each with a lid to hold in heat and keep out insects and dust. Your troop may have its own Boy Scout cook kits. If not, check secondhand stores and garage sales for good buys on used pots and pans. Complete the kit with a pair of hot-pot tongs for safely lifting pots and pans from the stove.

To carry cooking gear, divide the items among the members of your group. Save space by stuffing the pots with spare clothing or food packets before you put them into your packs. Carry large pots by slipping them over the ends of sleeping bags strapped to external-frame packs.

Cook kits may vary, depending on the type of camping your troop or patrol has planned.

A few utensils will help you turn out tasty meals with ease. Depending on your menus, consider taking a spatula, ladle, stirring spoon, vegetable peeler, and can opener.

Plastic Sheets. A couple of plastic sheets about 4 feet square can serve as clean surfaces for food preparation and equipment storage.

Water Containers. Besides individual water bottles, you may find it convenient to have a few collapsible plastic water containers for use in camp. Common container sizes are 1 gallon and 2½ gallons.

Cleanup Materials. Dishwashing is easier if you have the right supplies. Several soapless scouring pads, a rinse agent, and a little biodegradable soap will take care of most of your needs. A convenient way to stow pots, pans, and personal eating gear is by placing items, as soon as they are washed, in a small fishnet hammock strung between two trees, or in a mesh bag tied to a branch.

Trash Bags. Large plastic trash-can liners come in handy as storage sacks, as emergency ponchos and pack covers, and for suspending food on bear lines. They can also be used for carrying trash home at the end of a trip.

Pack Your Pack

You have planned a campout and gathered your food and gear. After loading everything into your pack, there should be little left to do except head out the door and let the adventure begin.

Besides your own gear, you probably will carry some group equipment. Your share might include several pots, part of a tent, a camp stove, and some food. Arrange soft items in your pack so they will cushion your back. Keep your rain gear, flashlight, first-aid kit, water bottle, and hike food near the top of your pack or in its outside pockets where you can reach them easily.

If there is room, stow your sleeping bag inside your pack. Otherwise, cover it with a ground cloth or a plastic trash-can liner to protect it from the elements. Tuck it under the pack's top flap, or strap it to the external frame. (Some Scouts put a trash-can liner inside a stuff sack first, then stuff the sleeping bag into it. The resulting bundle is neat, waterproof, and easy to pack.)

With everything in place, try on your pack. Is it comfortable? Does it feel balanced? Are the straps and hip belt properly adjusted? Are the items on the outside of the pack secured so that they won't swing around or fall off as you hike? Make any changes now so that you can hit the trail with a pack that is balanced, neat, and easy to carry.

Making Camp, Breaking Camp

Getting There

There are many ways you can travel to camp. Often you will hike in—perhaps a short distance, perhaps many miles. Your group may journey to a frontcountry camp by automobile, van, bus, or bicycle. Where lakes and streams abound, you may go in canoes or a raft guided with oars.

Many campsites can be reached with the help of a topographical map and a compass. The *Boy Scout Handbook* can provide you with guidelines for using a compass and a map to find your way. The *Fieldbook* and the *Orienteering* merit badge pamphlet contain more detailed information on route-finding in all kinds of terrain.

Global Positioning System

The global positioning system, or GPS, gives travelers a powerful electronic means of navigation. A GPS receiver small enough to fit in your pocket accurately calculates the longitude and latitude of any spot on the globe by taking bearings on satellites orbiting 12,000 miles above Earth. With it, you can identify where you are, plot a course to a campsite or other destination, and keep track of your elevation above sea level. As you move, you can program a GPS receiver to plot the record of your route, then use it later to retrace your steps.

Refer to the user's manual that comes with a GPS receiver to explore its many capabilities. Be aware, though, that just as having a calculator does not eliminate the need to know how to add and subtract, a GPS receiver (especially one with dead batteries) is no substitute for being able to navigate the backcountry with traditional tools. Develop confidence in your ability to use maps and compasses and then, if you wish, use them with a GPS receiver.

Selecting a Campsite

Much of the success of a campout depends upon the campsite you choose. A good place to camp offers plenty to see and do. Also, by following the principles of Leave No Trace, you can be sure your camp will be easy on the land.

Safety

Don't pitch a tent under dead trees or limbs that might fall in a storm. Stay out of gullies that could fill with flash floods. Find a site away from lone trees, mountaintops, high ridges, and other likely targets of lightning. Camp some distance from game trails, especially in bear country.

Size

A site must be large enough for members of your camping party to pitch their tents and cook their meals. When hanging food to keep it away from animals, find the trees you need at least 200 feet from where you will be sleeping.

Terrain

Does the site you have chosen for camp slope gently for good drainage? Leaves, pine needles, and other natural cover can keep the ground from becoming muddy. An area open to the east and south will catch sunlight early in the day and perhaps be drier than slopes facing north.

Privacy

Respect the privacy of others. Trees, bushes, and the shape of the terrain can screen your camp from trails and neighboring campsites. Keep the noise down when other campers are staying nearby.

Permission

Check well ahead of time with land managers of public parks, forests, and reserves. They can issue any permits you will need and may suggest how you can make the most of your campouts. Get permission from owners before camping on private property.

Water

You will need water for drinking, cooking, and cleanup—several gallons a day for each Scout. Public water supplies (faucets and drinking fountains) are safest and can often be found in frontcountry campsites. Water taken from streams, rivers, or lakes must be properly treated before use. Camping in dry regions can be very rewarding, though you must carefully plan how you will transport the water you need to your camp.

Open Water. Water taken from streams, lakes, and springs may contain bacteria and parasites too small for you to see. Treat any water that does not come from a tested source, using one of the following methods.

• **Boiling.** Bringing water to a rolling boil for a full minute or more will kill most organisms.

Treatment tablets can quickly lose their strength after a bottle has been opened. Find the date on the label and use only fresh tablets.

• **Treatment Tablets.** Water treatment tablets are sold in small bottles just right for hikers and campers. The label usually instructs you to drop one or two tablets into a quart of water and then wait 30 minutes before drinking. Tablets may leave a chemical taste in the water. After the tablets have had a full 30 minutes to do their work, you can improve the flavor by adding some drink mix.

• **Filters.** Camping stores and catalogs offer water treatment filters that are effective and easy to use. Some operate by pumping water through pores small enough to strain out bacteria. Others contain chemicals or carbon. Follow the instructions that come with the filter you plan to use.

Managing Your Campsite

Once you arrive at a site, the first order of business is to figure out the best way to settle in while causing little impact on the land.

• Set up a dining fly first. That will provide shelter for food and you in case of rain and will give a sense of where you will center most of your camp activities.

• Pitch your tents. Use established tent sites whenever possible. In bear country, tents should be 200 feet or more from the cooking area and from areas where food will be stored.

• Establish a plan for personal sanitation and be sure everyone understands what he is to do.

Sanitation

Getting rid of human waste outdoors requires special care. In campgrounds that have rest rooms or outhouses, be sure to use them. Where those don't exist, dig a cathole or use a latrine. Wash your hands with soap and water or use a waterless hand cleanser when you are done.

Cathole. Find a private spot at least 200 feet (75 steps) from water, campsites, and trails. Dig a hole 6 to 8 inches deep with your heel, a stick, or a shovel. Organisms in the top layers of earth will break down human waste. Fill the cathole with soil when you are done, and replace any ground cover. Push a stick into the earth to warn others against digging in the same spot.

Latrine. A patrol, troop, or other large camping group may be able to lessen its impact on the land by digging a single latrine rather than making many catholes. Check with a ranger or other local expert for guidance.

To make a latrine, use a shovel to dig a shallow trench a foot wide and 3 to 4 feet long. Remove and save any ground cover. As with a cathole, go no deeper than the topsoil so that waste will be buried in organic earth where it will turn into soil nutrients. Sprinkle a layer of soil into the trench after each use to keep away flies and hold down odors. Return all the soil to the latrine when you break camp, and restore the ground cover.

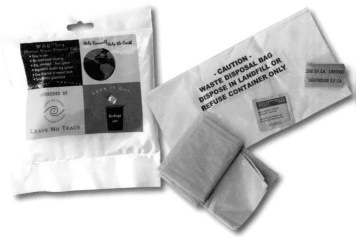

Cleaning Up After Meals

Whether you cook with a stove or over an open fire, put on a pot of water before you serve a meal. That way you will have hot dishwater by the time you finish eating.

Each person can wash his own eating gear. If everyone also does one pot, pan, or cooking utensil, the work will be finished in no time. Use hot-pot tongs to dip plates and spoons in the hot-rinse water. Lay clean utensils on a plastic ground sheet and let them air dry.

Begin cleanup by setting out three pots:

- **Hot-water wash pot**—hot water with a few drops of biodegradable soap

- **Hot-water rinse pot**—clear, hot rinse water

- **Cold-water rinse pot**—cold water with a sanitizing tablet or a few drops of bleach to kill bacteria

Dealing With Leftovers. Carry food scraps home in a trash bag. Don't bury leftover food or scatter it in the woods. Animals will almost always find it, and it is not healthy for them to eat. Food scraps can draw animals close to campsites where they may lose their fear of humans. That can be dangerous for them and for you.

Dishwater Disposal. For campouts lasting no more than a couple of days, use a small kitchen strainer to remove food bits from your wash water and put them in your trash. Carry the wash and rinse water away from camp and at least 75 steps from any streams or lakes. Give it a good fling, spreading it over a wide area.

For longer stays at one site, dig a sump hole at the edge of camp and at least 200 feet from streams, lakes, or other open water. Make the hole about a foot across and 2 feet deep. Pour dishwater through the kitchen strainer into the hole, or place a piece of window screen across the hole and pour the water into the sump through that. The strainer or screen will catch food particles so that you can shake them into a trash bag. Fill the sump hole when you break camp, and replace any ground cover.

Wash out jars and cans, and carry them home for recycling. Save space by cutting out the ends and then flattening cans.

Food Storage

Store your food where it will be safe from animals, insects, dust, debris, and bad weather. Frontcountry campers can use vehicles, coolers, or plastic buckets with tightly fitted lids as storage units. In the backcountry and anywhere that bears may be present, a bear bag is often the answer. Not only will your food be secured, hanging anything with an aroma will give bears no reason to linger in your camp.

Land managers of camping areas frequented by bears can give you further information about the best ways to store your food. Their suggestions may include using metal bear boxes or other storage canisters that cannot be opened by wildlife.

Here are three ways to suspend food and other "smellables."

1. Find a tree with a sturdy horizontal branch about 20 feet above the ground. Put a couple of handfuls of soil in a bandanna or plastic bag and secure it to the end of a 50-foot length of nylon parachute cord. Toss the weight over the branch. Stash your provisions in a sturdy plastic trash bag or waterproof stuff sack. Twist it closed and secure it to one end of the cord with a clove hitch. Pull the other end of the cord to raise the bottom of the bag at least 12 feet off the ground and 8 feet away from tree trunks—well beyond the reach of any bears. Secure the free end of the cord to a tree.

2. If there is not a good branch nearby, find two trees about 20 to 30 feet apart. Toss a line over a branch close to the trunk of one tree, then toss the other end of the line over a branch of the second tree. Tie your bear bag to the center of the line, and hoist it high between the two trees.

3. Bears accustomed to raiding campsites may be smart enough to claw loose the tied end of a cord. To prevent that, divide your provisions equally between two bear bags. Raise one up to a high branch, as you would in the first bag-hanging method. Tie the free end of the cord to the second bag and lift it overhead. Use a stick or hiking staff to shove it out of reach of animals. The bags will counterbalance one another, and your food will be safe. To retrieve the bags, use a stick to push one bag even higher, causing the other to come down within your grasp.

Fun in Camp

Setting up and managing a camp takes time, but there is more to camping in the outdoors than that. A campout can get you close to an area where you can enjoy an exciting activity— swimming, for example, or kayaking, photography, or environmental studies. As you plan a trip, think about the opportunities for adventure within easy reach of your campsite. Other possibilities include:

- Take a day hike to a lake, the top of a mountain, a scenic vista, or another point of interest.

- On winter trips, try cross-country skiing or snowshoeing. Build an igloo or a snow cave. Look in the snow for the footprints of wildlife, and follow them to discover the habits of different animals.

- Bike along trails open to pedaling.

- Go canoeing, rafting, or fishing.

- With proper supervision, take part with your group in organized climbing and rappelling activities. Learn the correct skills and safety procedures from qualified instructors.

Stormy Weather Camping

When the weather turns bad, your camping skills can be put to a real test. Draw on previous outdoor experiences and stay focused on the task at hand, and you should be able to make the most of a campout no matter what the clouds throw at you. Here is one way to go about it.

- First, look after your personal safety and that of your group. Take steps to stay warm and dry, and be on the lookout for signs of hypothermia.

- Secure your camp. If you have just arrived at a campsite, set up a dining fly and use it to shelter your gear while you pitch the tents.

- Fire up a camp stove, heat a pot of water, and soon you can lift everyone's spirits with hot drinks, bowls of soup, and other kitchen delights.

- Enjoy the outdoors while the weather rages. Storms bring with them a magic that you can't experience when the sun is shining.

- Be patient. You won't be able to change the weather, so there's no need to become upset even if the rain has cut short other outdoor activities.

Now and then there is nothing better than tent time in a storm. With a dry tent, a warm sleeping bag, and a good book, you can settle in for a few relaxed hours. Add good friends to share stories and games, and you will find that being weather-bound can be one of camping's great pleasures.

Don't forget that requirement 9c calls for you to perform a conservation project approved by the landowner or land management agency. Your merit badge counselor will be a good source of information as you plan and carry out your project. See the *Environmental Science* and *Soil and Water Conservation* merit badge pamphlets for ideas, too.

Breaking Camp

All good things must come to an end, and that includes camping trips. As you break camp, keep in mind these suggestions:

- Leave the dining fly in place until you are almost ready to go. It can serve as a last-minute shelter for people and gear.

- With the doors open, shake out the tents before stuffing them in their storage sacks.

- Check the locations of catholes and latrines to be sure they have been buried and ground cover has been restored.

- If you used an established fire lay, dig through the cold ashes. Remove and pack out any bits of food, metal, and other litter and trash.

- Inspect the areas used for cooking, food storage, and tents, and be sure you have picked up everything you brought to camp. Leave the campsite looking better than you found it.

Back Home

Going to just leave that pack on the floor when you get home? Taking care of your gear lengthens the life of your gear, too.

• Clean and air out all of your gear, including sleeping bags. Then hang up the sleeping bags or store them loosely in large cotton sacks.

• Set up tents or hang them from a clothesline or indoors.

• Wash your dirty clothes.

• Scrub all pots and pans clean.

• Brush any dirt or mud from your boots and treat them with boot dressing to keep the leather flexible and water-repellent.

Lastly, start planning another adventure. The next time you want to go camping—and it won't be long—you will already be well on your way to the great out-of-doors.

Giving Full Meaning to Camping

Whether you pitch your tent in the same place many times or you enjoy a campsite and then move on, everywhere that you sleep in the open becomes part of your personal outdoor history. You will be surprised over the years how often these adventures come to mind, and with what pleasure you remember the places that, at least for one night, you called home.

Camping is a central activity of the Boy Scout experience, and for good reason. It can bring out the best in everyone as groups of friends put their energies into practicing outdoor skills, solving problems, and having great times together. You can increase your understanding of personal health and safety, conservation, and the citizenship responsibilities of caring for the land. Most of all, camping allows your Scout spirit and the meaning of the Scout Oath and Law to shine through in all that you do.

Scout Oath

On my honor I will do my best
To do my duty to God and my country
And to obey the Scout Law;
To help other people at all times;
To keep myself physically strong,
Mentally awake, and morally straight.

Scout Law

A Scout is trustworthy, loyal, helpful, friendly, courteous, kind, obedient, cheerful, thrifty, brave, clean, and reverent.

Camping Resources

Scouting Literature

Boy Scout Handbook; Basic Illustrated Camping; Okpik: Cold-Weather Camping; Don't Get Sick; Leave No Trace; Passport to High Adventure; Fieldbook; Conservation Handbook; Topping Out; Backpacking, Bird Study, Canoeing, Cooking, Cycling, First Aid, Fishing, Fly-Fishing, Hiking, Mammal Study, Nature, Orienteering, Rowing, Small-Boat Sailing, Snow Sports, Whitewater, and *Wilderness Survival* merit badge pamphlets

Visit the Boy Scouts of America's official retail Web site at *http://www.scoutstuff.org* for a complete listing of all merit badge pamphlets and other helpful Scouting materials and supplies.

Books

Adare, Sierra. *Backcountry Cooking: Feasts for Hikers, Hoofers, and Floaters.* Tamarack Books, 1996.

Birkby, Robert. *Lightly on the Land: The SCA Manual of Backcountry Work Skills.* Mountaineers Books, 1996.

Forgey, William. *Basic Essentials: Wilderness First Aid,* 2nd ed. Globe Pequot Press, 1999.

Gorman, Stephen. *AMC Guide to Winter Camping.* Globe Pequot Press, 1999.

Graham, John. *Outdoor Leadership: Technique, Common Sense & Self-Confidence.* Mountaineers Books, 1997.

Hampton, Bruce, and David Cole. *Soft Paths: How to Enjoy the Wilderness Without Harming It.* Stackpole Books, 1995.

Harmon, Will. *Leave No Trace: Minimum Impact Outdoor Recreation.* Falcon, 1997.

Hart, John. *Walking Softly in the Wilderness: The Sierra Club Guide to Backpacking,* 3rd ed. Sierra Club Books, 1998.

Harvey, Mark. *The National Outdoor Leadership School's Wilderness Guide: The Classic Handbook.* Fireside, 1999.

Jacobson, Cliff. *Map and Compass,* 2nd ed., Basic Essentials Series. Globe Pequot Press, 1999.

McGivney, Annette. *Leave No Trace: A Guide to the New Wilderness Etiquette,* 2nd ed. Mountaineers Books, 2003.

Pearson, Claudia, editor. *NOLS (National Outdoor Leadership School) Cookery,* 4th ed. Stackpole Books, 1997.

Randall, Glenn. *The Outward Bound Backpacking Handbook.* Lyons Press, 2000.

Viehman, John, editor. *Trailside's Hints and Tips for Outdoor Adventure.* Rodale Press, 1993.

Organizations and Web Sites
Your local library, state parks, and state conservation lands may also serve as good resources for camping in your area.

U.S. Bureau of Land Management
Office of Public Affairs
1849 C St., Room 406-LS
Washington, DC 20240
Telephone: 202-452-5125
Web site: *http://www.blm.gov*

Florida National High Adventure Sea Base
P.O. Box 1906
Islamorada, FL 33036
Telephone: 305-664-4173
Web site: *http://www.bsaseabase.org*

National Park Service
Web site: *http://www.nps.gov*

Northern Tier National High Adventure Base
P.O. Box 509
Ely, MN 55731
Telephone: 218-365-4811
Web site: *http://www.ntier.org*

Philmont Scout Ranch
17 Deer Run Road
Cimarron, NM 87714
Telephone: 505-376-2281
Web site: *http://www.scouting.org/philmont*

U.S. Fish and Wildlife Service
1849 C St. NW
Washington, DC 20240
Toll-free telephone: 800-344-9453
Web site: *http://www.fws.gov*

USDA Forest Service
1400 Independence Ave. SW
Washington, DC 20250-0003
Telephone: 202-205-8333
Web site: *http://www.fs.fed.us*

Acknowledgments

The Boy Scouts of America thanks Robert Birkby, author of the 10th and 11th editions of the *Boy Scout Handbook* and the fourth edition of the *Fieldbook,* for his assistance in revising the Camping merit badge requirements and his work in revising the *Camping* merit badge pamphlet.

Thanks also to members of the BSA Camping Task Force for their practical and technical expertise: James Bean; James Blair; Jim Erwin; Marshall Hollis; William Kane; C. Mont Mahoney; Edwin Morrison, M.D.; Gene Schnell; David Shows, Ph.D.; and Darrell Winn.

The BSA is grateful to the Quicklist Consulting Committee of the Association for Library Service to Children, a division of the American Library Association, for its assistance with updating the resources section of this merit badge pamphlet.

Photo and Illustration Credits

Omega Studios—cover *(sleeping bag)* and page 35

©Photos.com—cover *(knife);* pages 13, 14, 18, 21, 31 *(top),* 50, 59, and 60

All other photos are the property of or are protected by the Boy Scouts of America.

Dan Bryant—pages 32 *(top),* 34, 36 *(bottom),* 51 *(top left),* and 52 *(top)*

John Fulton—cover *(pack)* and page 45 *(top)*

Daniel Giles—cover *(GPS receiver)* and page 56

Roy Jansen—cover *(compass)*

John McDearmon—page 4 *(both)*

Christian Michaels—page 7

Brian Payne—pages 22, 25, 29, 30, 45 *(bottom),* and 55

Randy Piland—pages 26, 46, 54 *(top),* and 57